INK AND INK AND FLESH AND LENGTH

INK AND INK AND FLESH AND LENGTH

ANNE F. WALKER

This edition published in 2025
By Eyewear Publishing Ltd.
The Black Spring Press Group
London, United Kingdom

Cover design by Edwin Smet
Typeset by Subash Raghu

All rights reserved
© 2025 Anne F. Walker

ISBN 978-1-915406-75-0

No part of this publication may be reproduced, stored in or introduced into a retrieval system or transmitted in any form or by any means, electronic, mechanical, photocopying, recording or otherwise, without the prior written permission of the publisher.

www.blackspringpressgroup.com

Contents

The Train to Water   9

     Ink and Ink and Flesh and Length   10

     Beating Heart of the Track   11

     Beating Heart of the Track   12

     Relentlessly   13

     All of it   14

     @Fifteen   15

     @Fifteen   16

     @Fifteen   17

     @Fifteen   18

     Driving   19

     Settling In   20

     Fields and Fields and Fields   21

     The Future   22

     The River Styx   23

Hometown Return   25

     Loosely Remember   26

     Elision   27

     Gattuso and Slaight Building   28

     Ninety-Nine-Year Land Leases   29

The Triggering Town	30
Good Use of Beautiful Light (on Clinton Street)	31
Good Use of Beautiful Light (on Clinton Street)	32
Good Use of Beautiful Light (on Clinton Street)	33
Good Use of Beautiful Light (on Clinton Street)	34
Good Use of Beautiful Light (on Clinton Street)	35
Good Use of Beautiful Light (on Clinton Street)	36
Good Use of Beautiful Light (on Clinton Street)	37
Good Use of Beautiful Light (on Clinton Street)	38
Good Use of Beautiful Light (on Clinton Street)	39
As if Through Fire	40
Yonge Street Mural	41
The Perfect City	42
The Perfect City	43
The Perfect City	44
The Perfect City	45
The Perfect City	46
Kaleidoscope Box	47
Sister and I Alike in Some Ways	48
Nickle and Dime	49
When the cat in the hat went to Hawaii, he took the fireplace and other things that felt	50
William	51

I Want to Tell You	52
I Want to Tell You	53
I Want to Tell You	54
Demeter's Country	55
Postcard found at the Ferry	56
Fan Letter found at the Ferry	57
9/11 Morning	58
9/11 Scheduled Meeting on Aristotelian Mimesis in Urban Poetics	59
You make me want to come home	60
Fix	61
Metalepsis Kiss	62
Metalepsis Kiss	63
Metalepsis Kiss	64

Demeter's Country   65

If Imagination Would Hold the Thread	66
Demeter's Country	67
Demeter's Country	68
all kinds of things moving around in the grasses	69
Pomegranate Seeds	70
Portable Hot Light	71
To Red Rock Beach	72
Red Rock Beach	73

Emerge.	74
Warm Springs	75
Three Wants	76
Glutted on a Morning Rose	77
Acknowledgements	78

THE TRAIN TO WATER

Ink and Ink and Flesh and Length

Mixing with the many Amish and Hutterites from their "Sail and Song" Alaska cruise is a tattooed couple that breathe each other like eyes read words to create worlds. Youth, beauty, fabulous fashion, and constant fall into one another's touch. Her American accent and his French. They sit on the same side of any table, touch when one leaves or returns as if they know the language of recognition. Her 1960's Woodstock gold-rim dark circle sunglasses. Her shirt falls to reveal a wife-beater falling to reveal a deeply tattooed body. His arms are ink and ink and flesh and length.

Beating Heart of the Track

Lights out through a tunnel, brief, unexpected. And back into light dry grassland. Repeat. Screen dims in sudden dark. Foothills before the Sierras. An old man with white skin and rosacea, skin that pulls back loose as he drinks beer in observation deck sun. *That's the beating heart of the track* the small blond boy drawing points out his picture to the young blonde freckled mom, tired between two small children. My family used to camp in gold country. This train, next to this river. I have seen this track and train from the road and thought *one day, maybe.*

Beating Heart of the Track

Last time through this high desert with Papa. We drove cross-country in his Element. Through Utah salt flats, him saying *I do not believe in forgiveness for some things*. To soothe I echoed *they did the best they could with what they had*. *But that's not true*, he said. Maybe about his own father, or mother. Or further back. Maybe about him letting me go when I was too young. There was that flat yellow-gold land for miles before the mountains' far distance, some brown abandoned wood-slat structure not far from the road. Water up over fences, telegraph wires falling.

Relentlessly

Water by the track is up over fences, and power poles struggle to stay up. The woman from Illinois in the diner car talked about her full moon night, coming down on the train from Seattle, said, *I just watched the river all night long*. She said she didn't sleep with the thrill of that to be seen. Me I'm watching the sun set and light go from the rocks and waters we cross relentlessly. Tunnels and grasses. Rivers overtaken by rains. Brief sleep. Woken by dreams of an earthquake in a high rise. The top floor swaying and rolling.

All of it

Wake from high rise earthquake dreams, the top floor swaying, rolling. At breakfast I miss my dad, miss pointing out antelope to one another, travelling the continent back and forth since I was little. I hold memories one by one, surprised by the grief. Ruby Canyon can only be seen by train or rapids. And this I have never seen. Colorado River swollen from a thick-packed snows' melt. Rafters ride brown water between red cliffs' strata. Parts are like Pacific sandstone's soft curves and hollows. I tell the blond artist in front of me. I tell him all of it.

@Fifteen

Failed out of grade ten for not enough classes. A daily over-the-counter codeine user since thirteen I hung out in the high school's bricked south exit to smoke between Physics, enriched Math, and Drama. All seasons. Painfully awkward I smoked to try and look tough. Slender hips curved under skin-tight lay-on-the-bed-to-zip-them-up Roadrunners. Black tee-shirts, part-laced tan cougar boots with jeans sticking out. Red cigarette box stuck out the left pocket of my jeans jacket. By winter I was drinking. And that set everything off. By the spring I took a bottle of pills, changed my mind, and told my sister.

@Fifteen

My solution was to buy the one-way ticket from Toronto to Vancouver with a loose plan that I would pick apples in the Okanogan Valley in British Columbia. My parents' solution was to drive me to the airport. The marathon runner once said they drove me to the airport like one twists the top off a vodka bottle then throws that top out the car window onto the highway. Nothing was going to be saved. Every bit would be drunk or spilled.

A lot was lost like a thick-knit Mexican sweater left on a rock in the stream when swimming.

@Fifteen

Just then leaving the hostess gig at Smitty's Pancake House in Banff after I'd been fired. On those mountain roads, in the clarity of sunlight and clear mountain air. That breath where I just felt somehow a fleetly neutral truth that I was still a child, and that I should not be out on the highway. With my thumb stuck out. That all my bravado was false. There isn't as much narrative to that memory. A moment like the morning light on a truck and the crisp shadow it casts. The moment moved by me, and I kept hurtling forward.

@Fifteen

At midnight. At the Sumas border. With what I remember to be a full moon shining through fog. Stoney gave me his knife, which I still have tucked away in a memory box. Without paperwork Lana and Stoney turned back into Canada and I headed forward into the States along the abandoned two-lane highway. After some kind of eternity that I remember as peaceful, an old truck came into view and I got my thumb out. It carried two men, and I got in. I remember some sense of awkwardness with them. We drove down that road to a town.

Driving

Constant push forward. I resist I resist I resist. Back through my mind I pull like a horse strains against reins. A white horse, gold reins. My head comes back close to my neck and shakes the mane. *I resist I resist.* Suddenly I am a memory of a car, driving through the 132, across the Central Valley to work. Six years of driving. That exhaustion. That place over the river awareness would wake, knowing there are undefined things of great volume outside the vehicle in which I travel. All stories in the dark by which I whisk in exhaustion.

Settling In

Unbelievably small roomette and a lounge car full of light. Full of people, fields, the bay the delta. Just stepping off and stepping in. I have crossed this country with my father, with my mother and sister. With my son and his father. Driven across with furniture as I migrated, first one way, then back. No Wi-Fi on this train. Lifting from Rosedale passing homes with green kidney shaped pools. Dry grassland. A smell of croissant moving through the cars before lunch. Voices waft in snippets, talk about a small round house, internet, taking the train, walking to a sale.

Fields and Fields and Fields

Knee high by the fourth of July, the new passenger says, *except for storms that ruined whole fields.* She looks out, *why don't they clean these windows? They're disgusting actually.* The Hutterite husband tries to explain his use of cell phones, cars, and electricity, finally shrugs a little, *it's how we were brought up. Don't you have things you do or don't do just 'cuz that's how it's done?* We all nod a little, feeling edges of small habits, turns toward or turns away on nothing but some invisible inside thread pulling. There's a flatness here, endless flat and green.

The Future

The muddy muddy Mississippi River the conductor says. We are about to cross it. And it is wide. We wait. The Burlington truss bridge is up to allow large boats to pass. The conductor narrates our wait with history, again calls it *the muddy muddy Mississippi River*. And then again. Rust colored riveted metal center truss lifts. A huge heavy machine. And then falls slow back to a low rise above the river. We cross. On the other side a dust brown train runs parallel to us for a while. Large white and dirty words read "How The Future Travels."

The River Styx

A soft slip of a woman in a rough neighborhood asks directions on the bus. The local man asks *what are you doing, going there?* She says, *I'm an alcoholic in town for a few hours, going to a meeting. I know the place,* he nods, names it, and gives instructions precise as pickets and bricks, fences and buildings, where to get off the bus, where to walk, how to return. The club is a biker-bar turned recovery-center, an old saloon painted matte-black, high metal ceilings. A large seated woman stays and talks, sighs, *heroin is... killing people 'round here.*

The River Styx

HOMETOWN RETURN

Loosely Remember

The placement of streets, neighborhoods how they were, houses before renovation. Sidewalk before a pail of soapy water is poured. Loosely streetcar rails. (The frame and) everything (outside the frame) disappears then reappears (as inside disappears): (a street meeting two others in a triangle where everything veers) black wires against blue sky along angles of streetcar tracks, everything sunbaked (like ghost images spilling from a broadcast t.v. channel, a figure behind the glass) disappears then reappears (as a girl on the sidewalk leans on a blue bike squints to see into the chromed greasy-spoon that hasn't changed in thirty-five years

Elision

Proportion between things in the house became unfamiliar. Wood bench longer from the wall as I remember it. Everything used to space perfectly to each other thing. Orange juice or skim milk in two-liter pickle jars. So many sleeping voices quiet this time of night. I remember poems more than geography. Outside the brick apartment to which Hank would bring beers to his baby's alcoholic mum, a slender millennial long-hair feeds a baby black bird in a cardboard box on the street. The bird slick and slow moving. Life at any cost. I buy flowers and fruit to bring home.

Gattuso and Slaight Building

Devastated by the news I walk and walk without a place to go. University Avenue is broad and I have been walking hours. Just past the embassy. In front of the hospital. Two women in red wide wheelchairs, thin white hair and brown patches on tissue-light skin, like Gramma. One is asked, again, if she wants to try the orange juice and is still unable to say *yes* or *no*. The other watches intently, neck curved from the weight of her tilted head. A man paces in small steps that stagger like brain injury. Back and forth. Back and forth.

Ninety-Nine-Year Land Leases

Crossing the bridge at the foot of Roncesvalles Christine remembers I would laugh about the rage woven in. All those years back. When sometimes I would hear in a whisper: *anger sometimes has no comfort. I think sometimes about sliding away out to the prairies, or that's the latest thought, the prairies. We. Have a calendar and it's April. The picture is of rolling meadows coated in ripe dandelion-like gauze and I think about going there sometimes and having no past.* The lake floods. Water from both sides of Centre Island has overtaken the shore and met in the middle.

The Triggering Town

Out of the way, let sound guide. Loud and busy on main streets, on Bloor from Yonge, sky-rises, high-end shopping. Money in and out of stores like smartly-dressed teenage girls' indifference. My accent now pronounced and foreign, I walk without a place to go. Around Dovercourt and Queen I stop where it started, where I'd hiked up a pink mini-skirt, pushed back Glenn's thin glass basement pane. A cop had stopped to ask if I needed help. *No,* I'd said with my suburban-girl smile, *just forgot my keys.* Inside I'd wrote a love-note on his shaving mirror in blue eyeliner.

Good Use of Beautiful Light (on Clinton Street)

Coffee comes in like a drug after sleeping dawn to dusk, waking to the faint amber line. Outside the kitchen door. Traffic sound hovers, amplified wasps. Oval skull of winter trees like yellow dye in veins. Silhouette of a couple of large apartment buildings a couple of miles away. Gas blue flame heats a silver percolator in the dark. A world of stars and darkness, like electric snow in a black and white television, the prickly black tugging though cool linoleum floor to pull back under, into dream. Reading all of Orwell's *1984* in one night, locked in the narrative.

Good Use of Beautiful Light (on Clinton Street)

Knowing it has something to do with me, locked in the narrative. When he turns to me a sun shines. Dusk falls when he turns away. I disappear into a Pavlovian dark: a mouth of childhood swallowing me whole. Invisibility sharp as winter air to lungs. There is always someone shoveling outside like a cough that cannot go. A chop of hockey sticks against concrete constant as the green rustling of high summer. Against sunset after sunset just hearing traffic and trees on a small street through an iced open window. When he turns back, I can breathe. Words ease.

Good Use of Beautiful Light (on Clinton Street)

Words ease. The third floor flat, second home with that husband, and the roof. Small bedrooms. Top of the house. Kitchen that let out to the flat tar roof. I recall: *Coming home, at Dundas West the satellite dish dark behind billboard before low rise window wall. A streetcar pulls into the platform's light. Deep red and oval windows above square windows. The yellow light inside. It's just before light. That blue. Tree leaves are still black in the wind. More cars pass. He grabs my wrists on the subway, holds too tight. A stiff hook corset under cobalt silk.*

Good Use of Beautiful Light (on Clinton Street)

Under dusk's cobalt silk. Out the kitchen window and door we catch the sunset in poems and scripts. The floor is beige linoleum shaped in large ugly tiles. It is winter and the sun sets by four-thirty. The time we awaken. Together up the scalable slope to the level. The first time up to the top he sits down flat when I get close to the edge, an edge that doesn't frighten me. Often he cannot stand, even in the center of the black tar, or see the view of downtown, or CN tower a ways away. Together we awaken.

Good Use of Beautiful Light (on Clinton Street)

Together we awaken. Onto the black tar roof with the back of the building behind us, a dark body. Together to the center. He stops. I walk toward the sheerness that falls away like life. That ends without announcement. I look over the thin edge, tingling from its closeness. Knowing it has something to do with me. Involuntary, his legs give out and he sits down where he had stopped. He cannot get up when I am that close to it. His legs will not. He cannot, breathe. Until I move toward him. He is lost in the swallowing hole.

Good Use of Beautiful Light (on Clinton Street)

The swallowing hole. He tells me about a high-rise in the eastern suburbs of Toronto. Him a teenager. His deaf brother lived in the building. Him on the roof with a friend. It's winter. Him fifteen and just out from a tiny town on Nova Scotia's cold eastern edge. Up on the high-rise skidded around on the ice covered roof with a powder snow as if back home by gentle slope to a small creak. Suddenly he could not stop. He lay down on his belly, slid closer and closer to the edge where people look small and indistinguishable below.

Good Use of Beautiful Light (on Clinton Street)

Small and indistinguishable below. The momentum stopped at the edge and his head looked over. Enough to scare one for life. Enough to make one sit down in the middle of the roof when one's love got close to an edge. I recall: *The biking away in tears. Him coming after me in rage. Him catching me.* I laugh at his fear, play with it, move toward the edge, watch him fall, and return to him so he can stand. Then back to the edge again to watch him fall. I recall: *Sounds so removed from the crying and fighting.*

Good Use of Beautiful Light (on Clinton Street)

I recall: *(two thin sheets of silver slide against each other magic rubbed invisibly between) Sounds so removed from the crying and fighting. How words eased the pain of one tearing into the other. And that terribly harsh numb as "one" and "the other" are he and I and have no words.* He falls and I laugh. Every single time he collapses. Every. Single. Time. A pain-in-throat-laugh harsh as winter air to lungs, as biking in flight. The prickly black threatening to pull me back under through cool linoleum floor, my tether, Pavlovian dark, mouth of childhood, swallowing me whole.

Good Use of Beautiful Light
(on Clinton Street)

I recall: *Gramma took me to the market down the roads from her farm and the river. Bought me a tiny wood horse made of slim tubes and strings that collapsed when my small fingers pressed under the circle base. The tiny horse popped up with the release. The simple pleasure of it. Watching the toy dissolve and stand again.* As if pressing my thumb on the wood toy I make him fall. Laughter out of control, a car without brakes on a low slow slope. A parked car suddenly without brakes. Suddenly brakeless it all has too much weight.

As if Through Fire

Steph and Christine sorted all the picture boxes, putting animals and landscapes in piles I could go through, labeling the rest. One old 60's picture was of the back of the old van. It was full of supplies and looked at first like another landscape variation. Steph then said *I bet this is when they took supplies to the farm workers Cesar Chavez was organizing*. We saved that one too. Gradually they helped me weed it down to seven generations of family photos and documents. I had come with only carry-on, so I bought a big hard suitcase in Toronto.

Yonge Street Mural

On Cathy's wild ride to Pearson she depicts being a singer on ships. Her little car lets out little honks now and then to see that others see her as she darts in and out of small spaces in the traffic's flow. From Pearson the photos come back with me in an overstuffed carry-on. I do not let smooth-dressed blue-dressed assistants check it, explaining several times that these were seven generations of my family's photos. Explaining a little about my dad's memorial. Eliding my sister. I carry them like a teddy bear who would keep away all the night fears.

The Perfect City

Some days are a stumble and want. Want to be in that other house, in that other city, where everything is okay. Mid 1960's Tante came to live in our 1904 farmhouse in downtown Berkeley. My mum said it was around when I turned two. We called her Tante, German for auntie. She was a gramma to me. When we got her I remember waking from sleep on the seat in the back of the old Ford van. Beige vinyl stuck to my skin in the seat's train-track patterns. Adults putting boxes in the back and Tante in the front.

The Perfect City

Her face looking something like an old white bird, there was a sharpness around her nose and some dark hollows around her eyes. She smoked and had mid-short wavy white hair. My parents closed the dining room on the first floor so her bed stretched past where the table had been. Behind the large kitchen and pantry back windows faced out over the yard, doghouse, and apricot tree. A closed porch behind Tante's room seemed to be all screens and boards. A bathroom at its far left was fitted with a shower that had sturdy handrails so she wouldn't slip.

The Perfect City

There were vague memories, a physical sense that she was in her room in that house. Corduroy pillows with arms helped her sit up comfortably in bed. My mom told a story about me walking with a pencil between my fingers as if it were a cigarette. I had explained that I was practicing to be a Gramma. I was heartbroken when we left her in California as we moved to Canada. When she died she left me a black-framed mirror, a box of things that included her wedding ring, her magnifying glass for reading, and her 1920's cigarette holder.

The Perfect City

The most precise memory really starts with racing through the kitchen to get to the porch bathroom on time. Running with small-child bowed legs. The seriousness and stress of that sprint through the house to make it. Maybe two-years-old. As I came up to the screen door, very clearly, seeing through the kitchen door to Tante's room. And she was beaming at me. She clearly adored this little person caught in that urgency and in mid run. I don't remember her saying anything, or my awareness slowing me down. This unexpected moment of being completely cherished, as I hurtled by.

The Perfect City

When I remember her, and particularly that moment of her adoring little me earnest in my running, it makes me wonder if Tante was right and my mom, dad, and sister weren't. What if I am that beloved little girl simply because I am. Because I exist and do the things that one does because one is. Not because I have done any right thing, simply because I exist. That's what I want. In everything. It is exactly what I want. When I want to escape and find that perfect city where everything is okay, it feels like Tante's love.

KALEIDOSCOPE BOX

Sister and I Alike in Some Ways

As a little kid in Oaxaca I saw people stare. Once, in the Mercado's thick push of people, close to the stall of leather purses, Mother said folks looked because of my blue eyes. Grampa and Uncle on Mother's side had blue eyes. Sister's were brown. She is older. My bones strong and Sister's were not. I loved jumping off a second story, rolling onto grass, racing up the fence and coach house parapet to do it again for the feel of the fall. I had to stop when Sister's leg broke falling off a couch. Her bones were delicate.

Nickle and Dime

Cousin was a dime and I was a nickel. I knew that before words. Two small hard things in one hand. She was the girl her mother wanted enough to endure five pregnancies, two miscarriages. Small and slight, her mother dressed her like a doll. I was the family problem. The colic, the wouldn't-stay-on-the-blanket. The unbreakable blamed when sister broke bones easily. The reason professor told my mom to leave grad school, my mother told me, that I bent her ribs out. Cousin was the princess. Me, cinders, the fuzz-black duckling, the ugly. Something others wanted away from. Worth less.

When the cat in the hat went to Hawaii, he took the fireplace and other things that felt

like home, you repeat. Then talk about the hotel the cat isn't sure about, the odd pool below. Blonde hair wild again. Your father comes, and you can't stop telling the story. I say *you can tell me the rest on Skype*. You say *Yes*. And keep telling the story as your father instructs you to put on one worn black velvet high-top, and then the other. You stagger into each shoe, breaking it a little more than before. You keep telling the story, all the way out to the black truck, from which you wave as it drives away.

William

89-year-old hands shake. My sister pours his ritual tea into small fragile cream-white cups with watercolor-blue lines. He puts two blueberries on the worn unfinished wood deck railing. This little porch by the green palm forest he had grown over forty years from a desert of broken rocks. As we talk a small red bird comes for one blueberry. I ask about poetry. He wants to talk about real things, animals, how we treat them. He wants to tell me about Topsy the elephant, and the puppy he had briefly before his parents took her while he was at school.

I Want to Tell You

about heat today. The smell of bleach and flowers in Au Coquelet. The smell of flowers. The feeling of waiting and not rushing. The man behind the counter moves slow to come get my order. Ice decaf Americano. There are places I want to show you. A garden metal fountain at the Alano club, covered with flowers. The smell, and the music and the pause, all in the heat of the air. Cuban Salsa by the Malecón, waves crashing underneath. It's not really that I want to show you, it's that I want to immerse you in it, with me.

I Want to Tell You

that my favorite X-Man is Jean Grey because of her hot smart nerdiness, red hair, and that she turned into Phoenix. That she didn't know. I don't know still how much is inside me. I want to believe there is more than I can imagine. I just want to tell you about how hot it is today, about a month ago, more than two hundred black plastic chairs in the church hall, and I laid down cut-off black gloves with pink skeletons patterned in on two near the front. For Trisha and me. We left the heat of the church.

I Want to Tell You

Trisha and me left to eat and talk outside on the stone wall where it's cool by the street. When we come back the room is filled, and we sit where I'd put down cut-off black gloves with pink skeletons patterned in. Nine years in a world that has expanded and contracted precisely since you and I were eye to eye. And there you are next to Trisha. When you hear about the 80s dance about to happen you lean forward on your black plastic folding chair, look at me and say *do you know how to do The Bump?*

Demeter's Country

California turns dry in summer, my mother told me, *because Persephone is in the underworld,* stolen by Hades. The first captivity. Pomegranate seeds. A mother broken by rage and sorrow halts seasons. Living things cease to grow, and die. I see hillside grasses turn from green to the gold-grey of lion-fur. *We live in a Mediterranean climate,* my mother would say, and I understand we live in the old myths. I wonder what languages draw these threads of stories between time. My teeth hold the tight membrane around red juice circling those small seeds. Brittle like shell, white and yoke.

Postcard Found at the Ferry

Susan, repulsive blue metallic dragonflies fluttered over a repulsive lake. Rust brown from industry. Frothing. She insisted we lay in the water, in its froth and steam of an intake from who knows where. She said the inheritance depended on it. Oddly, it felt lovely on my toes, between them. Like the jet from a hot tub, a redwood hot tub resting in 1000-year-old trees. But cool, not cold, cool. It focused my mind. My body lifted against water's odd chemistry. She claimed it was the blood of Jesus anointing us and without that, nothing would be anything. Yours, Rebecca

Fan Letter Found at the Ferry

Known to eat Mars bars and drink diet coke, to play Bowie, to move to music on the scraped Plexiglas dancefloor, its neon rainbow lit from underneath in rhythm below a fog of footstep scuffs. Bryan's slender presence could not compete with your grace, angular face, divided eyes and genre-theft. We could spend your last hours anywhere, talk art and I could show you my blue electric car. I wouldn't care that you are old. That I am old. I would attend to you, memorize you like song. I would write you and sing you quietly until my throat hurt.

9/11 Morning

Slim calls early because I don't have a tv. Jamil is showering and needs to be at middle school soon. Like a cloud passes a full moon I quietly hope it will all blow over before he gets out. I don't know how to narrate this. Grief pools in my throat as I hear water stop running. At Slim's we watch small figures falling live, grainy on the tiny black and white tv that gets broadcast images from its wire hanger jammed in. Dropping black specs seem almost unreal. But they are not. I can feel that they are not.

9/11 Scheduled Meeting on Aristotelian Mimesis in Urban Poetics

On the way up to school I hear live radio. A witness reporter describes first responders going up stairwells in ways that create the sounds of steps, people running up concrete while others run out. Clamor. Asked, *what happened to them*, there is no pause, a beatless Q&A. *They can't have made it out* he says and I hear him understand what he says as he says it. A horrible pause and push. He tries to keep speaking his job. In the book-lined office facing east Professor says she is worried about the war that will come out of this.

You make me want to come home

to put out the cigarette by the laundry machine. Your eyes are not the same, odd and deep. A chiasmus of tying, untying. At night I fall in the tunnel of dreams between us: *You smell my breath in the hot tub for cloves or cigarettes. Wearing your huge orange clothes I billow, still you reach and pull, like thick green fish packed thick together on the green dresser a small child painted. The clumsy blue fish big and small packed in and out of one another like needles knitting and yarn, or multiple overlapping mumbles of voices in prayer.*

Fix

Things don't stay solid. The pictures you sent me last week are now old. Your invitation two nights' past has not born fruit. Even though I know I know I know. You're away with your family by the cool deep ocean in a house that stretches over the shallows. Sunlight flickering all across to the inlet's other side. The pictures are old; things are not solid. I'm thirsty or hungry, I can't tell. I need something, something to make me feel different. My hands want to hold clay, your hands, some deep despair dressed as a gymnast in a car.

Metalepsis Kiss

I sure hope this sweetness is not like the ant bait that kills those critters slowly, in the kitchen this weekend. It's a day where everything does not pack away neatly. Fireworks over the freeway overpass, where a figure runs, a shadow running. Fast I pass below the mesh-fence darkening the darkened sky, and the figure running, the shadow running. Fast leaving the Berkeley Marina's absurdly low firework show. There's been a lot of stories this week running loud as trucks through my head. I don't know if it's a snapdragon, or a redwood tree, growing between our growing being.

Metalepsis Kiss

You find a wind hollow in the fine light sand, warm light sand supporting dune grasses, a blue Mexican blanket, our two bodies. You ask me to define three blues at magic hour over the lake: the water in the crescent closest to the columns is slate, the next line out to the edge is indigo, and sky over the city, over the freeway above the end of the water, is turning marine and approaching night. This kiss in the car. You kissed me before you kissed me. On the walk you say *you look cute in pajamas*. Word kiss.

Metalepsis Kiss

You text:
> *Meet me where heart and fingers of God intersect.*
> *Angel of blue skies touches your skin.*

I got out to Pacifica to encounter heavy rain. As that cleared a lightning storm just hovers over the ocean miles out and the sun just too hot on the humid beach. In July. Crazy. The lightning keeps coming down from that frightening grey as one that spikes into two over the dark-blue-turning-green ocean. In July you become the one I want to speak with. I am telling you all this in a dream, so tonight we can just be in tonight.

DEMETER'S COUNTRY

If Imagination Would Hold the Thread

The airplane ride a long crushing base of upright spine and chair that won't recline. Spanning night's continent. The couple watch a space romance on small screens in front of each seat, share two earbuds, lean over narrow armrests that don't lift, as if escaping something inside the body by fleeing into the other's. I wonder if a thin surreal string that held our red balloon has frayed over thousands of miles. I imagine our red balloon pulls at the back of this airplane through a crack in the window, rises toward grey white clouds, a lightning storm, its end.

Demeter's Country

This is Demeter's country. Persephone's still locked away the other side, and it is dry. Dry grass, air. Deep long train whistles across miles. Steady chug of wheels. We adapted. Created countries that live over top each other, bounded by hills and salt water, bridges. Tents group under freeways. Or fill sidewalks. Sometimes who-knows-who throws kerosene lamps to burn them down. People line up on street-corners for work and wait all day there, just in case. Stark as stick huts and dirt floors the other side the river of my youth. Expensive cars drive over top the raised concrete scars.

Demeter's Country

Persephone sleeps below. Hills and city dry. One murmurs, *it's earthquake season* as if we could know by the creak of the sky. We adapted. Internet money and coders move from the old city to this one. Boutiques, restaurants, hospitals, like any nation above Hades. Without rain green grows on ocean's early mist. Marine layer, in each morning. Sweet wild alyssum and honeysuckle all over. Purple jacaranda, tulip trees green under pink and white opening flowers, palms, gardens with water piped from Sierra reservoirs. Hetch Hetchy, Pardee, Camanche. We forget Demeter. Her sorrow and sleep. Her presence holding back rain.

all kinds of things moving around in the grasses

man & boy chasing the white goat & the slight river water making that bell-sound so far from what you said to me & me taking that which you said the same way the small green plants nestle into that sand & root, as if you were some earth for me in which i awaited the end of this drought that turns mountains brown, chaps lips, i nestled into you like a river bed where sand was alive & people migrated over, i nestled into you like the sky into the hollow between hills on which ancient ruins lie buried

Pomegranate Seeds

Metal-emerald hummingbirds drink one at a time, pause before the light waterfall. Long beaks stretch into cool water in unseasonal heat like large hovering insects that then dart back-and-forth across the redwood gully. Steps away from the whole rest of the moving world. You bring a cream blanket, wood cutting board, white plates, glass glasses and metal straws, ice, sparkling water, mint and lime. Into this heat. A blue dragonfly comes to rest briefly on the silver spoon. You create and plate a many-part meal as if singing in a language I don't speak. I follow the song. Its melody.

Portable Hot Light

Where sound and sense coalesce in this illuminant that pulls forward from the near-empty expanse of cabin by Donner Lake. You move through the photographs in potentia, lighting them from angles impossible in one moment. Shuttering so many shots from the solid tripod, each glistens or glows from a different source. As you cast light. As you hold light in your hand. As you stab with it into corners to create glints intuition will pull from and layer in post-production. Sifting through electronic levels as if lifting tissue paper: draft after draft. An old architecture of coalescence. Sound and lit.

To Red Rock Beach

I don't think you notice. As if a fog about us—you tell me about loss, moving forward, a long slow cold and distance, ex-wife's *want to make things better*, your *that it never was*, and *could not be*. We turn together to this passage. After examining the white trail that steeps up and over, the uncertain flatter lower rocks with unknowable distances between serrated edges, we slow toward the low. Where goat-like I used to find small places for my hands and feet, projecting forward lithely, I now falter. Over and over you reach a hand to steady me.

Red Rock Beach

An unease of ocean, large waves, and of undertow pulling out to sea. Close to our towel the young slender couple dances half-dressed in invisible music. The wide ocean opens its wide mouth and waits.

You strip and dive in. You are a seal.

I'm slow.

Cold, you find the beach, the towel I lent you. The sun. I stay in waves, slight waves that carry less as I feel the long slow sloping sand beneath my feet does not drop off. Immerse so the crown of my head feels the cold. Emerge. I feel you watch. Again and again.

Emerge.

You dry naked on the beach when I return with menthol skin almost prickling from salt and cold. For a while we lie side by side. Arms touch slightly. I seek that warmth, skin, light touch. I tell you then what it is I want, side by side with you. The late sun lowers and air begins to cool. Scaling boulders back I berate myself (quietly internally) for fear of aging and of doing so alone. Fear that one misplaced step will fall me between rocks and sudden blood. Just past where the electric cars park and charge for free.

Warm Springs

Remi Grace is fifteen months and long and strong next to the stream where small coho salmon dart in lines that look like art on a canvas. The many and their shadows beneath in shapes like arteries into veins, or systems of roots growing at the speed of water. Remi Grace on the green lawn next to hula hoops. I pick up one wrapped in green and pink and blue ribbons. Let it circle me. She runs toward me and I stop. Let it down to her height. Her small hands hold on from inside and she laughs, practices jumps.

Three Wants

1. The tulip tree budding on Colusa at noon. A fine rain collects on the windshield lit red by brake lights. What more evidence do I need of grace: your white hair and imperfect gait.

2. I use you as tin to God. A reflector set up in the desert, a microwave dish. I lie out in the sun of it. Tin can with a string through it in an old black and white movie or TV show. I call Creator through you. I lay atop your shine and pray.

3. All the glass air around me ready to shatter.

Glutted on a Morning Rose

The sky is busy with shooting stars, the milky way, sound of running water. Several at a time, flashing red lights of west-bound cross-continent planes span the Sierras. Last week I was on one, still sleeping. Fitful. Unaware of the huge chirping night below. The bottom of an ocean risen. I can't shut my eyes to it.

Moths or night-flies buzz around the lit tent. Trying to fan, to thump, to thump, into the glow of the solar lantern my beautiful son lent. Like you, I too have been broken. And put back together, light shining through so many seams.

Acknowledgements

Grateful thanks to Maw Shein Win, Connie Hale, Dawn Trook, Peggy Morrison, and Trisha Peck for detailed editing support. Thank you Susan P., Jennifer S., Chimmed D., and Jenny and Scott T, for your love, support and guidance. Thank you Auntie. Thank you Todd Swift, Black Spring Press Group, and Catherine Myddleton-Evans for careful consideration, supporting the poetry in this book, and bringing it out into the world. Thank you so much to Jamil for always giving me a reason to keep going.

'Pomegranate Seeds' and 'The Triggering Town' were published in *Cloudbank 12*.

Six poems from *Ink and Ink and Flesh and Length* were also used in a multi-media event hosted in the Bay Vista Room at Holy Names University in Oakland, California. Titled *the beating heart of the track,* Dawn Trook's contemporary performance art integrated Andie Vas' visual art and music by Antonio Domenick. Misha Bruk photographed through magic hour and into night.

The second *the beating heart of the track* interactive performance was designed by Dawn Trook and again based on the poetry from this collection. The performance included readings, images-in-motion by Trook, spontaneous music by Devina Jimenez, and visual art by Tonya Lopez-Craig and her Conceptual Art Class from the University of California, Merced. Photographers entered the space as tourists as part of the performance, stilling the bodies in motion. The Merced Multicultural Arts Center graciously housed the event.

'To Red Rock Beach' was printed in *Mary: A Journal of New Writing*.

The manuscript's writing was supported by a Poetry Fellowship from the Martha's Vineyard Institute of Creative Writing and a Faculty Development Award for Writing from Holy Names University. It was shortlisted for the Sexton Poetry Prize with Eyewear Publishing.

Finally, I extend great appreciation to the English and Comparative Literature department of San José State University for holding a nourishing creative teaching environment, and to the community offered by the San Francisco and Berkeley Page Street Co-Working Spaces for Writers.

I no longer feel like an island.